ANNE GEDDES™

Copyright © 2000 Anne Geddes
www.annegeddes.com
The right of Anne Geddes to be identified as the Author
of the Work has been asserted by her in accordance with the
Copyright, Designs and Patents Act 1988.

First published in 2000 by Photogenique Publishers
(a division of Hodder Moa Beckett)
Studio 3.16, Axis Building, 1 Cleveland Road, Parnell
Auckland, New Zealand

Published in Great Britain in 2000
by HEADLINE BOOK PUBLISHING
A division of the Hodder Headline Group
338 Euston Road, London NW1 3BH

10 9 8 7 6 5 4 3 2 1

Produced by Kel Geddes
Colour separations by MH Group

Printed by Midas Printing Limited, Hong Kong

All rights reserved. No part of this publication may be reproduced, stored in
a retrieval system, or transmitted, in any form or by any means without the prior written
permission of the publisher, nor be otherwise circulated in any form of binding or cover
other than that in which it is published and without a similar condition being imposed
on the subsequent purchaser.

British Library Cataloguing in Publication Data
for this title is available on request.

ISBN 0 7472 7267 0

*The publishers are grateful for the permission to reproduce those items
which are subject to copyright. While every effort has been made
to trace copyright holders, the publishers would be pleased to hear from
any they were unable to contact.*

ANNE GEDDES
Thoughts with Love

Addresses

Name

Address

Fax/Email

Phone(s)

Name

Address

Fax/Email

Phone(s)

Name

Address

Fax/Email

Phone(s)

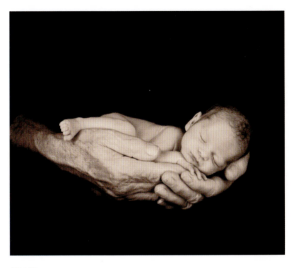

We can do no great things – only small things with great love.

Mother Teresa (1910–1997)

Name

Address

Fax/Email

Phone(s)

Name

Address

Fax/Email

Phone(s)

Name

Address

Fax/Email

Phone(s)

Name

Address

Fax/Email

Phone(s)

Name

Address

Fax/Email

Phone(s)

Name

Address

Fax/Email

Phone(s)

Name

Address

Fax/Email

Phone(s)

Name

Address

Fax/Email

Phone(s)

Name

Address

Fax/Email

Phone(s)

The smiles of infants are said to be the first fruits of human reason.

Rev. Henry N. Hudson

Name

Address

Fax/Email

Phone(s)

Name

Address

Fax/Email

Phone(s)

Name

Address

Fax/Email

Phone(s)

Name

Address

Fax/Email

Phone(s)

Name

Address

Fax/Email

Phone(s)

Name

Address

Fax/Email

Phone(s)

Name

Address

Fax/Email

Phone(s)

Name

Address

Fax/Email

Phone(s)

Name

Address

Fax/Email

Phone(s)

A mother understands what a child does not say.

Proverb

Name

Address

Fax/Email

Phone(s)

Name

Address

Fax/Email

Phone(s)

Name

Address

Fax/Email

Phone(s)

Name

Address

Fax/Email

Phone(s)

Name

Address

Fax/Email

Phone(s)

Name

Address

Fax/Email

Phone(s)

Name

Address

Fax/Email

Phone(s)

Name

Address

Fax/Email

Phone(s)

Name

Address

Fax/Email

Phone(s)

$\mathcal{E}$ach day I love you more ... today,
more than yesterday ... and less than tomorrow.

Rosemonde Gérard

Name

Address

Fax/Email

Phone(s)

Name

Address

Fax/Email

Phone(s)

Name

Address

Fax/Email

Phone(s)

Name

Address

                              Fax/Email

Phone(s)

Name

Address

                              Fax/Email

Phone(s)

Name

Address

                              Fax/Email

Phone(s)

Name

Address

Fax/Email

Phone(s)

Name

Address

Fax/Email

Phone(s)

Name

Address

Fax/Email

Phone(s)

*L*ife itself is the most wonderful fairy tale.

Hans Christian Andersen (1805–1875)

Name

Address

Fax/Email

Phone(s)

Name

Address

Fax/Email

Phone(s)

Name

Address

Fax/Email

Phone(s)

Name

Address

Fax/Email

Phone(s)

Name

Address

Fax/Email

Phone(s)

Name

Address

Fax/Email

Phone(s)

Name

Address

Fax/Email

Phone(s)

Name

Address

Fax/Email

Phone(s)

Name

Address

Fax/Email

Phone(s)

There are only two lasting bequests
we can hope to give our children.
One of these is roots; the other, wings.

Cecilia Lasbury

Name

Address

Fax/Email

Phone(s)

Name

Address

Fax/Email

Phone(s)

Name

Address

Fax/Email

Phone(s)

Name

Address

Fax/Email

Phone(s)

Name

Address

Fax/Email

Phone(s)

Name

Address

Fax/Email

Phone(s)

Name

Address

Fax/Email

Phone(s)

Name

Address

Fax/Email

Phone(s)

Name

Address

Fax/Email

Phone(s)

Babies are such a nice way to start people.

Don Herold (1889–1966)

Name

Address

Fax/Email

Phone(s)

Name

Address

Fax/Email

Phone(s)

Name

Address

Fax/Email

Phone(s)

Name

Address

Fax/Email

Phone(s)

Name

Address

Fax/Email

Phone(s)

Name

Address

Fax/Email

Phone(s)

Name

Address

Fax/Email

Phone(s)

Name

Address

Fax/Email

Phone(s)

Name

Address

Fax/Email

Phone(s)

Name

Address

Fax/Email

Phone(s)

Name

Address

Fax/Email

Phone(s)

Name

Address

Fax/Email

Phone(s)

Name

Address

Fax/Email

Phone(s)

Name

Address

Fax/Email

Phone(s)

Name

Address

Fax/Email

Phone(s)

Name

Address

Fax/Email

Phone(s)

Name

Address

Fax/Email

Phone(s)

How soft and fresh he breathes!
Look! He is dreaming! Visions sure of joy
Are gladdening his rest; and, ah! who knows
But waiting angels do converse in sleep
With babes like this!

Bishop Coxe (1818–1896)

Name

Address

Fax/Email

Phone(s)

Name

Address

Fax/Email

Phone(s)

Name

Address

Fax/Email

Phone(s)

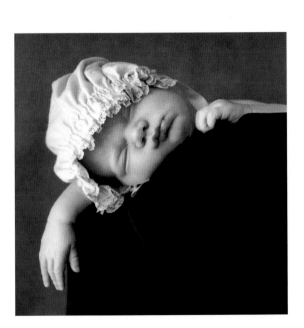

Name

Address

Fax/Email

Phone(s)

Name

Address

Fax/Email

Phone(s)

Name

Address

Fax/Email

Phone(s)

Name

Address

Fax/Email

Phone(s)

Name

Address

Fax/Email

Phone(s)

Name

Address

Fax/Email

Phone(s)

Name

Address

Fax/Email

Phone(s)

Name

Address

Fax/Email

Phone(s)

Name

Address

Fax/Email

Phone(s)

From small beginnings come great things.
Proverb

Name

Address

Fax/Email

Phone(s)

Name

Address

Fax/Email

Phone(s)

Name

Address

Fax/Email

Phone(s)

Name

Address

Fax/Email

Phone(s)

Name

Address

Fax/Email

Phone(s)

Name

Address

Fax/Email

Phone(s)

Name

Address

Fax/Email

Phone(s)

Name

Address

Fax/Email

Phone(s)

*O wonderful, wonderful,
and most wonderful wonderful!
and yet again wonderful.*

William Shakespeare (1564–1616)

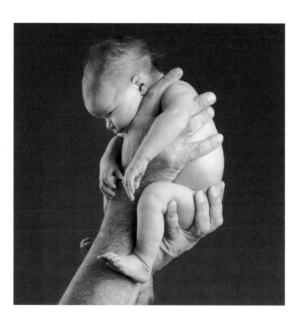

Name

Address

Fax/Email

Phone(s)

Name

Address

Fax/Email

Phone(s)

Name

Address

Fax/Email

Phone(s)

Name

Address

Fax/Email

Phone(s)

Name

Address

Fax/Email

Phone(s)

Name

Address

Fax/Email

Phone(s)

Name

Address

Fax/Email

Phone(s)

Name

Address

Fax/Email

Phone(s)

Name

Address

Fax/Email

Phone(s)

I have spread my dreams under your feet;
Tread softly because you tread on my dreams.

W. B. Yeats (1865–1939)

Name

Address

Fax/Email

Phone(s)

Name

Address

Fax/Email

Phone(s)

Name

Address

Fax/Email

Phone(s)

Name

Address

Fax/Email

Phone(s)

Name

Address

Fax/Email

Phone(s)

Name

Address

Fax/Email

Phone(s)

Name

Address

Fax/Email

Phone(s)

Name

Address

Fax/Email

Phone(s)

Name

Address

Fax/Email

Phone(s)

The very pink of perfection.

Oliver Goldsmith (1728–1774)

Name

Address

Fax/Email

Phone(s)

Name

Address

Fax/Email

Phone(s)

Name

Address

Fax/Email

Phone(s)

Name

Address

Fax/Email

Phone(s)

Name

Address

Fax/Email

Phone(s)

Name

Address

Fax/Email

Phone(s)

Name

Address

Fax/Email

Phone(s)

Name

Address

Fax/Email

Phone(s)

Name

Address

Fax/Email

Phone(s)

A new baby is like the beginning of all things –
wonder, hope, a dream of possibilities.

Eda J. Leshan (1922–)

Name

Address

Fax/Email

Phone(s)

Name

Address

Fax/Email

Phone(s)

Name

Address

Fax/Email

Phone(s)

Name

Address

Fax/Email

Phone(s)

Name

Address

Fax/Email

Phone(s)

Name

Address

Fax/Email

Phone(s)

Name

Address

Fax/Email

Phone(s)

Name

Address

Fax/Email

Phone(s)

Name

Address

Fax/Email

Phone(s)

You should have a softer pillow than my heart.

Lord Byron (1788–1824)

Name

Address

Fax/Email

Phone(s)

Name

Address

Fax/Email

Phone(s)

Name

Address

Fax/Email

Phone(s)

Name

Address

                        Fax/Email

Phone(s)

Name

Address

                        Fax/Email

Phone(s)

Name

Address

                        Fax/Email

Phone(s)

Name

Address

Fax/Email

Phone(s)

Name

Address

Fax/Email

Phone(s)

*It was the Rainbow gave thee birth,
And left thee all her lovely hues.*

William Henry Davies (1871–1940)

Name

Address

Fax/Email

Phone(s)

Name

Address

Fax/Email

Phone(s)

Name

Address

Fax/Email

Phone(s)

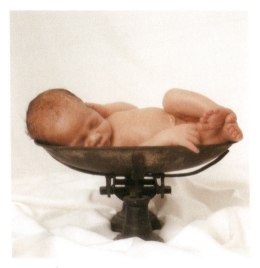

A perfect example of minority rule
is a baby in the house.

Anonymous

Name

Address

Fax/Email

Phone(s)

Name

Address

Fax/Email

Phone(s)

Name

Address

Fax/Email

Phone(s)

Name

Address

Fax/Email

Phone(s)

Name

Address

Fax/Email

Phone(s)

Name

Address

Fax/Email

Phone(s)

Name

Address

Fax/Email

Phone(s)

Name

Address

Fax/Email

Phone(s)

Name

Address

Fax/Email

Phone(s)

Small is beautiful.

Proverb

Name

Address

Fax/Email

Phone(s)

Name

Address

Fax/Email

Phone(s)

Name

Address

Fax/Email

Phone(s)

Name

Address

Fax/Email

Phone(s)

Name

Address

Fax/Email

Phone(s)

Name

Address

Fax/Email

Phone(s)

Name

Address

Fax/Email

Phone(s)

Name

Address

Fax/Email

Phone(s)

Name

Address

Fax/Email

Phone(s)

Do you believe in fairies?
... If you believe, clap your hands!

J. M. Barrie (1860–1937)

Name

Address

Fax/Email

Phone(s)

Name

Address

Fax/Email

Phone(s)

Name

Address

Fax/Email

Phone(s)

Name

Address

Fax/Email

Phone(s)

Name

Address

Fax/Email

Phone(s)

Name

Address

Fax/Email

Phone(s)

Name

Address

Fax/Email

Phone(s)

Name

Address

Fax/Email

Phone(s)

Name

Address

Fax/Email

Phone(s)

Tears ... the diamonds of the eye.

Rev. Dr. Davies

Name

Address

Fax/Email

Phone(s)

Name

Address

Fax/Email

Phone(s)

Name

Address

Fax/Email

Phone(s)

Name

Address

Fax/Email

Phone(s)

Name

Address

Fax/Email

Phone(s)

Name

Address

Fax/Email

Phone(s)

Name

Address

Fax/Email

Phone(s)

Name

Address

Fax/Email

Phone(s)

Happiness is the intoxication produced by the moment of poise between a satisfactory past, and an immediate future, rich with promise.

Ella Maillart (1903–)

Name

Address

Fax/Email

Phone(s)

Name

Address

Fax/Email

Phone(s)

Name

Address

Fax/Email

Phone(s)

Name

Address

Fax/Email

Phone(s)

Name

Address

Fax/Email

Phone(s)

Name

Address

Fax/Email

Phone(s)

Name

Address

Fax/Email

Phone(s)

Name

Address

Fax/Email

Phone(s)

*The decision to have a child is to accept that
your heart will forever walk about
outside of your body.*

Katharine Hadley

Name

Address

Fax/Email

Phone(s)

Name

Address

Fax/Email

Phone(s)

Name

Address

Fax/Email

Phone(s)

Name

Address

Fax/Email

Phone(s)

Name

Address

Fax/Email

Phone(s)

Name

Address

Fax/Email

Phone(s)